Advance Praise

"You will never think the same about immigrant workers and their children after you read these poems. And you will better appreciate the passion, frustration, pain and joy of those who teach English as a second language. A remarkable achievement in a few words."

— Newt Gingrich, 58th Speaker of the U.S. House of Representatives

"Meet Hala, Alma, Fazilah, and Fernan – just a few of the ESL students who populate the poems of World Class – and you will find yourself in a world as full of surprises as English itself. Elkin manages to capture the amusing without poking fun and to embody the heartbreaking without resorting to pity. Instead she employs the strong rhythms of accentual verse to explore what it is like to teach and to learn from students whose stories span the globe."

—Sue Ellen Thompson, author of *The Golden Hour* and winner of the 2010 Maryland Author Award

"This short collection of brave and honest poems is a powerful "poetry of witness" to a segment of America often overlooked and occasionally reviled. Elkin's accentual rhythms give insistent voice to the haunting stories of her hardworking and determined students, many of whom have fled horrors in their countries of origin in search of an elusive American dream. These poems will move you and stay with you."

— Anna M. Evans, editor, Barefoot Muse Press

"Elkin has given us a glorious gift by transforming beautifully written words into a moving yet mystical journey. This stellar compilation of poems takes us inside the secret world of strangers to our land while allowing us to pause for tea then find a comfortable quilt before reading each one over and over again! Not since Langston Hughes' "I Too, Am America" has there been such a deep emotional bond with those planted so firmly on the 'outside'."

— M.D Johnson, author of *The ISIS Project* book series

World Class

Poems Inspired by the ESL Classroom

J. C. Elkin

Apprentice House
Baltimore, Maryland

Copyright © 2013 By J.C. Elkin

All rights reserved. No part of this book may be reproduced or transmitted in any form or by any means, electronic or mechanical, including photocopy, recording, or any information storage and retrieval system, without prior permission from the publisher (except by reviewers who may quote brief passages).

First Edition

Printed in the United States of America

ISBN: 978-1-62720-002-8
Ebook ISBN: 978-1-62720-003-5

Design by Gina Brandon
Cover photo by Gina Brandon

Published by Apprentice House

Apprentice House
Loyola University Maryland
4501 N. Charles Street
Baltimore, MD 21210
410.617.5265 • 410.617.2198 (fax)
www.ApprenticeHouse.com
info@ApprenticeHouse.com

Contents

1	Introduction & Acknowledgments
5	Foreign Soil
6	World Class
8	Hala
10	Adios Fernan
11	Greeting Card Lesson
12	JoySong
13	Verdad Confronts the Truth
15	Young Means "Forever Unchanging"
17	Alma Works It Out
19	Abdalia
21	Fazilah Succumbs
23	The ABCs of Abeel Chinar
25	Françoise In Exile
27	PazMaya Under Pressure
29	About the Author

Introduction & Acknowledgments

I dedicate this work to my students, past and present, at Anne Arundel Community College. Their names, nationalities, and some occupations have been changed, but their circumstances as portrayed in these narratives are real. The quotations are as exact as memory permits.

Most of the poems are composed in accentual verse, a traditional form that stresses the rhythm of language, just as I do in the classroom. It dates back to the roots of English poetry, from Beowulf to folk ballads, and endures in the verses of children's rhymes and rap.

This collection would not have been possible without many sharp eyes and sympathetic ears. Thanks to the Broadneck Writers' Workshop – Simon Ward, Crystal Walker, Jeanne Slawson, Hank Pugh, Jessica Paret, Patsy Helmetag, John Clark, Shaun Bevins, and Iain Baird – for their helpful critiques throughout the writing and editing process. Thanks also to my coworkers for their encouragement, and to my husband for his unflagging patience and support, technical and otherwise.

In E.S.L. class
where new friends can't converse, they
hold hands, beaming joy.

First published in Serving House Journal (Fall 2011). http://servinghousejournal.com/
AmSenIssue4.aspx. Reprinted by permission of the publisher.

J.C. Elkin

Foreign Soil

My students arrive in dust storms of change.
Denims, saris, suits. All ages
from Persia's Gulf to Ganges' banks,
desert sands, Andes' peaks.
Blood red, rank, poor lands,

carrying seeds of rich loam,
through arid, rocky, barren years,
acclimating, blooming in time,
soaking up language's Miracle Gro.

They till the words until the words
that prick their ears at last make sense
sprouting from their tongues in accents
lush as rustling crop leaves.

World Class

"They should speak our language or just go back home."
That's what some folks say when they hear strange tongues.
Accents thick as hummus. Tortured broken grammar.
I once thought that way, before I lived abroad.
I know how it feels to be the alien.

Now I teach them English. "Tribal", "slanty-eyed",
Slavic, "rag-head" strangers, my heroes and friends
who put their lives on hold for twelve long hours a week,
asking probing questions, aiming for the A.

"What is mean, I feel sheety?" Her boss expects her to know.
Different forms of past tense. "I cannot say I had went?"
Just when they think they know, our grammar shifts beneath them.

They come to school for three hours after working night-shift,
cat nap, pick up the kids, cook dinner, start again.
They walk to the laundromat and scour flea markets for deals.
They grow humongous squash and divvy it out like sweets.
They're businessmen, janitors, cooks with stories you never would guess.

A father kidnapped for ransom because he has kids in the States.
An engineering degree wasted at Chick-Fil-A.
A kid who left Korea pursued by the Red Chinese
and sixty years later recalls the date he last saw his mom.

A genius from Cameroon who'll graduate high school soon.
His father, also my student, who still cannot read.
A guy who left school in third grade shrugs like it doesn't matter.

J.C. Elkin

"We needed money," he says. The easy smile of youth
that has all the time in the world. Another rues fortunes lost
on college diploma scams, still pursuing the dream.

I'm proud to say I help. Ashamed I don't do more.
I helped one girl find work. Tough work, but she recalls
her mother butchering dinner, cooking tamales from corn
she grew in her garden and ground to cornmeal on a flat stone.

She speaks of agrarian life without a trace of nostalgia.

Hala

Hala is my mirror,
the woman I might have been.
Hands on the small of her back,
she teeters down the hall.
We're both of a certain age,
married with grown kids.
Teachers learning to cope
with aging bodies' betrayals,
but hers put mine to shame.

My nagging sciatica
versus her arthritis.
My niggling heartburn,
her gnawing ulcers.
My cold hands and feet,
her Reynaud's Disease
triggered by stress and cold
from huddling twenty years
by a charcoal brazier
in urban one-room schools.

Promoted to Superintendent
of girls' schools in Peshawar,
she got the VIP treatment
that could have paid for heat.
She had a limo driver.
I chauffeur myself.
She had a secretary.
I have my PC.
She had an employee
who turned document pages
when she signed her name.
I make my own copies.

After Hala left home,
Malala was shot in the face
for exercising her right
to an education.
Nine million girls there her age
have never been to class.

My meager murmur.
Hala's broken heart.

Adios Fernan

Fernan wears his cap Gangsta-style.
Tall and strong and proud
and much less sure than he looks.
He stays after class with questions,
too shy to ask in class.

A waiter who can't take orders,
he thrusts his notebook at me.
"What drinks you want? You write."
It's more command than request
but his smile is pure gratitude.

One day he stays to tell me
he must go bury his mom.
Home to El Meximala.
Who knows when he'll return –
if he ever returns.
I don't know if he's legal.

I picture him sprinting at night
trying to cross the border.
Mentally cheer him on,
though once I'd have been livid.
When did I change my mind?

Vaya con Dios, my friend.
Your seat is empty today
but will be filled tomorrow
with another young dreamer.
The wait-list is long as the fence.

J.C. Elkin

Greeting Card Lesson

As young Fernan mourns his mother, we mourn his departure.
A sympathy card is in order. Time to decipher Hallmark.
A lesson I've put off for years because it seemed less important
than gerunds, infinitives, syntax, spelling, pronunciation....
Fernan's amigo, Juan, will see that the card finds its way.

We brainstorm reasons for cards and visit Bluemountain.com.
I explain why a thank you note I received at semester's end
wasn't quite apropos, engraved with the words *Be well soon*.
This class is quick. They smile, then grow solemn again
faced with new words like grief, loss, eternity.

Twenty-five strong we troop to Food Lion on a field trip.
The students wander Aisle Three judging the cards more by pictures
than by the words inside. They vote. The pink Ode to Mom
beats out the blue Vigil Prayer that Juan buys on his own.

The cashier pales at our mob, paging for back-up help.
"Don't bother," I say. "We're together." I hand him cash and the card.
Bae, a retiree who left his mom as a teen, waves me aside and pays.

Some stragglers stop to buy snacks they press on me during break:
Rice Krispie treats and seaweed we munch in quiet communion,
sensitive to our loss, grateful for this day together.

JoySong

There's a new girl, an Asian beauty.
JoySong does nails at the mall.
Her little boy lives with an auntie
while she pursues the dream.

She radiates wisdom and calm.
Smiling and shy and smart.
Aunties from neighboring nations
jostle to sit with her.

Her husband doesn't need school,
fluent in four-letter words
he utters as easy as "Bye"
each time he drops her off.

One day, I see as she leaves,
my textbook is packed in her bag.
She's more ashamed than embarrassed
when I remind her it stays.

Next day her arms are bruised.
Perfect dark fingerprints.
And I wish I'd just swallowed
the price of one more lost book.

J.C. Elkin

Verdad Confronts the Truth

"What is beach?" Verdad asks,
suspicion crimping her eyes.
"My son learn this word at school.
  I think it is not good."

"Bitch," I correct her, nodding,
writing it on the board.

She taught little kids in Peru.
Homeschooled all her children
until this one entered the mainstream
wolf pack of middle school.
Now it has come to this.

"A bitch is a female dog."

She ponders this, confused.
Reddens when she gets the gist.

"It's bad," I say, "very bad.
You're right to be concerned."

She wrings her hands, distraught.
"What am I to do?
  He needs English, yes,
  but this I do not expect."

I worried, too,
when my kids were young.
Assure her he'll be fine,
hoping I am right.

Good mothers everywhere
fret about their kids.
Her boy's beyond her grasp.
How fast can she learn to swear?

Young Means "Forever Unchanging"

Of all my ESL students,
Young is the one I can't reach.
No sense of syntax at all.
Random words tumble from him
like poetry magnets, in heaps,
and he's lost most of the verbs.

"Me restaurant eating friends."
Every day is the same.
Holding his paper at length.
Adjusting, wiping bifocals.
Adopting a thoughtful pose.
Copying words like a monk.
Perfecting each faint letter.
Always a question behind.
Sometimes on the wrong page.

Words crowd his mouth like marbles
slipping under his tongue.
I model. He interrupts.
I shush him. Tell him to listen.
Two, three, four times,
"I went out to eat with friends"
until a stranger just might
understand what he says.

One day I ask the whole class,
"What do you say to someone
  who's done something nice for you?"

Twenty blank stares reply
in thunderous incomprehension.

World Class

Only Young knows the answer,
parroting my exact words
for each of his many gifts
of candy and flowers and fruit.
"Thank you so much," he says.
Good manners are his forte.

That Christmas we celebrate
with an international feast.
The best student speaks for the class.
Gives me a card, a gift,
heartfelt simple thanks.

Then Young, not to be outdone,
stands and recites four words:

"Warm teacher.
  Born teacher."

Now I'm the speechless one.

First published in a different version by Poetry Matters Celebration (2013 Contest Winners). http://poetrymatterscelebration.com/2013-winners/. Reprinted by permission of the publisher PRA.

J.C. Elkin

Alma Works It Out

Alma stopped coming to class soon after changing jobs.
Was I wrong for helping her to make the switch?

She hated cleaning at Sam's.
Part-time. Minimum wage.
Worst possible hours.
No benefits at all.
I saw she was depressed,
overweight, lacking a goal.

Then her amiga came
with a tip that couldn't wait.
She gave me the number, eyes pleading.
I said she'd have to call.

"I am escare to talk."

I coached her in a speech
after school that same day.
"My name is Alma Perez.
 I'd like to apply for a job
 as a school janitor.
 I can start right away."
Shaking, out of words,
she passed the phone to me.

The system was convoluted. We had to apply online,
deciphering schedules and forms, using her child's email.
She dusted off references from a tattered notebook.
She scoured her brain to recall ten years' work history.
She inventoried her skills. We polished her resume.
One thing was clear to me – Alma was right for the job.

World Class

The day that she got the call
you'd think she'd just won the lotto.
Sixty percent pay increase.
Full benefits. Good hours.
For her it would mean the difference
between surviving and living.

But it was hard to master.
Nobody else spoke Spanish.
Ebonics was Greek to her.

I urged her to hang in there.
But she disappeared.
Six months I fretted for her.
Had she quit? Moved back home?

Then she came back, triumphant,
svelte in new clothes and a grin.
She thanked me — two, three times.
"I am so very happy,
 and is all for you."

My pay day comes early sometimes
without any check at all.

Abdalia

Chapter Two: Occupations.
Present Tense of the Verb To Be.

I am a teacher.
You are a chef.
He is a gardener.
What do you do?

driver, inspector, restaurateur,
housewife, beautician, roofer, cashier,
delivery boy, TV producer.
We practice saying these words just right.
Let's hear that "S".
It's an "L", not an "R".
Remember the word "a" or "an".

Abdalia, smiling gap-toothed giant,
stands and nods his assent.
At six foot five and three hundred pounds,
he's not someone you'd forget.
In clipped African accent he states
with pride, "I am a stocker."

He's dark as night,
strong as chloroform,
quiet as creeping death.
His job is a bad homonym.

I write S-T-A-L-K-E-R on the board.
I ask if he knows what that means.
Using the phone as a prop, I pretend
to call a girl in the front row.

Worshipful comments. Heavy breath.
Vague, inaudible whispers.

She laughs and squirms. Covers her face.

"Abdalia, if I were you," I advise,
"I'd say I'm a stockroom worker."

At the end of the day, he's still laughing.
I am a stand-up comic.

J.C. Elkin

Fazilah Succumbs

Fazilah slumps at her desk,
black nylon hijab a puddle,
only her black-hennaed fingers
peeking out from the veil.
Thirty-four going on fifty,
this woman's nearly worn out.

"Excuse me," she says with a sigh.
"I am not eating or drinking
  all the day while I fast."

August here is steamy,
weeping from every pore.
Fazilah knows desert heat,
but this is Ramadan.

"Not even water?" I ask,
hoisting a one-liter bottle.
I will drink three today.

"No. No," she says, "only small sips."

I struggle to hide indignation.
As if it weren't enough
she rises at four to cook,
walks everywhere in the heat,
swathed in oppression and sweat.

"I'm used to it," she says.
"Just give me a minute to rest."

World Class

I keep my phone at the ready
to call 9-1-1 if she swoons.
I thought I was tolerant, but
watching her melt in submission,
I hate her religion today.

J.C. Elkin

The ABCs of Abeel Chinar

When Abeel Chinar comes to class,
his favorite comedy schtick
is greeting classmates in accents
that mimic their speech. Quite a trick.

When he sees a pretty young girl,
he gawks from behind his notebook,
unable to turn away,
unable to take a good look.

When I return papers face-down
and leave the room on an errand,
Abeel Chinar turns them over,
unaware he might offend.

When I call on students in turn
and ask him to please remain quiet,
he talks with his hands, as if mute.
I scold, but think he's a riot.

I thought I was done teaching kids
but Abeel Chinar's a reprise.
At thirty-two going on twelve,
he embodies the ABCs.

World Class

A for Afghan refugee.
He lost the best years of his life
in relocation camps.
No schooling, no job, no wife.
Amblyopic. ADHD.
Attention-starved. Aimless.
A perennial adolescent
who nevertheless is blameless.

B for blushing boy-child.
Blessed with moxie and wit.
Braggart who claims to know all,
though nearly illiterate.
Bound up in Muslim tradition.
Birthright of favored first son.
Spent his whole youth being told
he was better than everyone.

C for computer whiz
solving my technical trials.
Wanna-be teacher's pet.
Courteous helper, all smiles.
Cock-eyed and callow and cursed
by war's ill-timed circumstance.
Only fit for class clown.
Given up hope of advance.

Rich by immigrant standards,
his dad drops him off in a Lexus.
Then one day, he's not there.
Someone said they moved to Texas.

Class is suddenly calm.
Too calm and ordered by far.
We all pine for the boisterous character
known as Abeel Chinar.

J.C. Elkin

Françoise In Exile

She strolls in, mid-lesson, scrolling text messages on her phone.
A has-been Olympian crowned with corn-row laurels.
The class bristles annoyance. It's the third time this week.
I remind we start at nine. I tell her to hang up the phone.

"Is Okay. Not to worry."

I tell her it's not okay – to put away the phone.

"Yes, in a minute," she says, waving away my voice.

I repeat in my *don't-test-me* tone.
She complies with a stony stare.
Saunters to the back row.

I take her aside during break, speaking in English
and French – just to be perfectly clear.

"This is America.
　Unlike in Côte d'Ivoire,
　here, we start on time."

She says she lives far away.
"The bus is leaving so early."
She doesn't like alarms, but "Is okay. Not to worry."
She says she'll come when she can.

I think about breaking my vow to welcome one and all.
"Be here by nine," I say, "or do not bother coming."

"Is okay," she repeats,
her eyes contradicting her lips.

World Class

I never see her again.
I don't worry. I think she's okay.
And I can't say that I miss her.
The wait-list is full of contenders.

J.C. Elkin

PazMaya Under Pressure

Lesson Six, Leisure,
seems like a cruel joke to me.
For most of my students, a day
at the beach is as good as it gets.

We practice *frequency adverbs*
in hypothetical skits:
How often do you eat out?
PazMaya, sighing, says,
"Never. I don't have time."

She works double shifts at McDonald's.
A widow supporting a clan:
her mother who's dying of cancer,
her daughter-in-law who stays home
to nurse her and tend to five kids –
Their father was shot to death.

This woman's ripe for a breakdown,
playing dodge ball with her health.
I wish I could pamper her.
How good a massage would feel
or a shopping spree for herself.

But I can't adopt every problem,
and she can't make time to eat out.
Besides, she might be insulted –
this dynamo who comes to class
with Valentine truffles for me,
brimming with questions that prove
she will never ever give up.

First published in Kansas City Voices (Volume 11, 2013). Reprinted by permission of the publisher *Whispering Prairie Press*.

About the Author

J.C. Elkin is a graduate of Bates College, Southern Connecticut State University, and the Defense Language Institute. Founder of The Broadneck Writers' Workshop, she is a Pushcart Prize nominee whose work has been recognized by Poetry Matters, The Poetry Society of New Hampshire, and the Maryland Writers' Association. An E.S.L. instructor at Anne Arundel Community College, she also works as a theater critic and singer, and makes her home on the Chesapeake Bay.

Visit Jane's webpage at
http://www.broadneckwritersworkshop.com/jane-c-elkin.html

Apprentice House is the country's only campus-based, student-staffed book publishing company. Directed by professors and industry professionals, it is a nonprofit activity of the Communication Department at Loyola University Maryland.

Using state-of-the-art technology and an experiential learning model of education, Apprentice House publishes books in untraditional ways. This dual responsibility as publishers and educators creates an unprecedented collaborative environment among faculty and students, while teaching tomorrow's editors, designers, and marketers.

Outside of class, progress on book projects is carried forth by the AH Book Publishing Club, a co-curricular campus organization supported by Loyola University Maryland's Office of Student Activities.

Eclectic and provocative, Apprentice House titles intend to entertain as well as spark dialogue on a variety of topics. Financial contributions to sustain the press's work are welcomed. Contributions are tax deductible to the fullest extent allowed by the IRS.

To learn more about Apprentice House books or to obtain submission guidelines, please visit www.apprenticehouse.com.

Apprentice House
Communication Department
Loyola University Maryland
4501 N. Charles Street
Baltimore, MD 21210
Ph: 410-617-5265 • Fax: 410-617-2198
info@apprenticehouse.com • www.apprenticehouse.com

www.ingramcontent.com/pod-product-compliance
Lightning Source LLC
Chambersburg PA
CBHW070454050426
42450CB00012B/3274